Never Cry Alone

NEVER CRY ALONE

CYNTHIA D. GRIMMETT

Library of Congress Cataloging in Publication Data

Grimmett, Cynthia D.
Never cry alone / Cynthia D. Grimmett
ISBN 0-9643303-0-X

Dedication

Many thanks to all my friends and family who welcomed my writing as a very young child and called it a gift. Thanks to those who shared the times which I was inspired to write about. A special thanks to my cousin who showed her support by putting my words into pictures.

I'd like to thank my mom, Lenora, for sacrificing her life as a beautiful, young, single parent to the successful rearing of her three girls. For teaching us to keep God first in our lives. For taking the time to listen to each one of us and accept our individuality. For instilling in us her unbreakable strength to accomplish whatever she set out to do, yet still maintain a gentle, generous, kind heart to all. For showing us how to live happy lives and more importantly how to love completely.

It is for these reasons that I dedicate this book to my mother. I love you, Mom.

CONTENTS

INTRODUCTION

If only we could look into our future when we are young to see what lies ahead, then we would realize that life is a cycle. Whatever is happening has happened before; whatever has happened will happen again. Thus, by life's experiences, we are continually being taught and made stronger persons.

Since we cannot look into our future, how can we be helped to cope with the trials that are being thrown at us? Think about this: why is it that the older we get the wiser we seem to become? It is a fact that wisdom and maturity come with the growing process. That being the case, through the experiences of those older than ourselves, we may be helped to deal with the problems that we are facing right at this moment.

Sometimes we feel that no one can understand what we are going through, how deeply we are hurting, how upset we are, how scared we are, how embarrassed we are. We put ourselves in an isolated category from the rest of the world—our problem is different; our problem is unique. Yes, each problem we encounter, each pressure we are confronted with is indeed unique in its own way. How so? In that the characters involved include you. It is no longer a situation that you just heard about: it is now reality and you have to make a decision.

When I told my dad I had written a book, he asked me what the title was. I told him NEVER CRY ALONE. He said he had no problem crying alone because every time he told his problems to someone they always ended up crying louder than him—with their own problems. That is truly the case many times. However, oftentimes we will find that when we cry out to someone they end up crying along with us. Why is that? Because they understand what we are going through; they understand how we feel. They are not feeling sorry for us but rather are being reminded of their own hurt, their own disappointment, their own injustice, their own failure: thus they cry along with us for they remember their own pain.

So never feel that others won't be able to help. Talk to someone—anyone. We will be surprised to find that many people are willing to listen to our tears. We so eagerly share our joy with others but keep our pain inside us to slowly eat away at us. Try sharing your feelings of despair with others. It is then that we will discover that even the people we admire the most, the ones we look up to, the ones we view as strong, unbreakable people have once in their lives been victims of hurt, pain and rejection. Everyone has a story to tell.

In my book NEVER CRY ALONE you will find brief vignettes followed by poetic summations. Feel the love, tears, hurt and pain and know that it can all be made easier by sharing it with others. Remember life is a cycle and therefore life goes on and on...Don't be left behind.

ASSUMED LOVE

The relationship had reached its fourth year. During this time certain commitments were expected but none had been made. Allan's actions proved that he cared. The things he would do for Michelle went far beyond mere friendship. Still, Michelle could not get rid of that gut feeling that Allan was uncomfortable in the relationship. Not knowing whether he was turned off by the thought of a long term relationship, or whether it was something about her that he was dissatisfied with made Michelle yearn to hear Allan say he cared.

Allan had never been able to express his feelings verbally and until now Michelle accepted this fact as part of his shy nature and in turn she had not felt the need to express her feelings for him. But lately things had changed. Assuming that Allan loved her was not enough. She needed assurance. She wanted proof. She longed to hear him say he loved her. Hearing this only once would satisfy her craving. Finally she realized that he would never say how he felt voluntarily so she gave him this prompt...

Say The Words

WHY CAN'T YOU LOOK INTO MY EYES
AND MAKE ME PROUD
OH DON'T YOU SEE I'M BEGGING YOU
TO SAY THE WORDS OUT LOUD

I THINK YOU REALLY WANT ME
AND NEED ME TOO
BUT WHAT I THINK IS NO GOOD
UNTIL I HEAR IT FROM YOU

I SUPPOSE I COULD JUST TELL YOU
AND YOU'D THINK IT TRUE
BUT IT COULD ALL BE MADE SO EASY
IF THESE WORDS I HEAR FROM YOU

HOW DO YOU FEEL ABOUT ME?
I'M DYING I HAVE TO KNOW
SHOULD I WAIT A LITTLE LONGER
OR PACK MY HEART AND GO?

MAYBE FIRST I'LL PUT MY GUARD DOWN
AND JUST TELL YOU HOW I FEEL
MAYBE AFTER I HAVE TOLD YOU
THEN SAY THESE WORDS YOU WILL

I KNOW SOME THINGS NEED NOT BE SAID
UNSPOKEN WORDS ARE SWEET
BUT TO HEAR YOU SAY THIS ONLY ONCE
WOULD MAKE MY LIFE COMPLETE

I LOVE YOU, I NEED YOU
YOU MAKE LIFE FOR ME SO REAL
TO HAVE YOU, TO HOLD YOU
A DREAM YOU FULFILL

Victim Of My Heart

"Yield not to temptation" and yield Doug would not but the temptation remained as did the desire to tell Keisha how he felt about her; however, there were certain circumstances which he felt restricted him from openly expressing those feelings.

As time passed, Doug's heart became filled. Realizing that by allowing himself to continue dwelling on these feelings it could eventually cost him a good friend, he tried hard to get rid of these desires.

Doug soon resorted to sending Keisha a letter explaining his 'newly discovered' feelings for her. Trying hard not to cause this victim of his heart any embarrassment by unloading his emotions on her, Doug chose his words very carefully. Here is what he said to Keisha...

To Fall For A Friend

THE LAST THING THAT I WISH TO BE TRUE
IS TO HAVE MY ACTIONS TROUBLE YOU

BUT HEARTFELT EMOTIONS YOU CANNOT CONCEAL
SO I MUST TELL YOU HOW I FEEL

WHEN I NEED SOMEONE JUST TO TALK TO
I WRITE A LETTER AND SEND IT TO YOU

WHEN I FEEL THROWN AGAINST THE WALL
I PICK UP THE PHONE AND GIVE YOU A CALL

WHEN I BECOME A BOTHERSOME PEST
I LEAVE YOU ALONE TO GIVE YOU A REST

WHEN I THINK A VISIT IS LONG OVERDUE
I INVITE YOU OVER SO I CAN SEE YOU

I COOK, I CLEAN, I WINE AND DINE
I TRY TO GET YOU OFF MY MIND

BUT OTHER THINGS JUST CAN'T COMPARE
WITH HOW I FEEL WHEN YOU ARE THERE

IF WISHES AND DREAMS COULD EVER COME TRUE
I'D WISH TO DREAM OF BEING WITH YOU

I'D WISH TO HAVE YOU BY MY SIDE
TO FILL A VOID I HAVE INSIDE

AND AFTER I'VE HAD MY FANTASY
I'D WISH SOMETHING IN REALITY
(continued)

FOR YOU TO BELIEVE THAT EVEN THOUGH TOLD
OVER MY FEELINGS I HAVE CONTROL

THAT I UNDERSTAND IT TO BE UNDERSTOOD
KEEPING THEM LOCKED IS FOR MY OWN GOOD

WISHES AND DREAMS THAT'S ALL PRETEND
THE REAL TRUTH LIES IN BEING A FRIEND

Who Loves A Star?

The city was filled with excitement. Headlines flourished. People waited eagerly in anticipation of the big event. Shopping malls were packed with books, records, clothes and videos; while the street vendors covered food, posters, stickers, tee shirts and any other imaginable item that could promote the upcoming visitor.

Lines formed over a mile long. There was very little pushing or unruly conduct. Newsmen were impressed at the cooperation of the crowds. Ticket salesmen added their appreciative tone to the situation they had beforehand dreaded.

The show was finally on. The two nights of breathtaking performances proved that the audience had been satisfied to the greatest extent possible. After the show, the crowds gathered outside in hopes that their insatiable desire to actually touch the star could also be filled.

Cameron, Renald and Selina were all distant spectators. Selina feared large crowds and for that reason they stayed at a safe distance. For as far as they could see, the crowd was pretty orderly, only screaming the star's name as the police-escorted vans approached them. Cameron and Renald had almost convinced Selina to move a little closer when suddenly the mood of the crowd changed. The previous crowd was transformed into a vicious mob who with only manpower stopped the moving van with the star in it! Unable to calm the mob, the bodyguard of the star said that if the crowd would move away from the van, the celebrity would get out and speak to them. There was almost instant response! As promised the star got out and stood on top of the van.

Selina borrowed Cameron's binoculars to get a closer look at the scene. She was saddened by what she observed. She saw the very humble superstar kneel down and shake the fans' hands, smiling warmly at them. Girls and guys alike were falling onto the ground and pulling their hair, screaming and crying.

Selina then began to feel a little sympathy for the celebrity. It looked as though the star would actually come out into the crowd if they would allow it. It was then that the three began to think about how stars lived their lives. Did they live secluded lives because they chose to or because we force them to with our innocent ignorance?

On the way home, Selina shared these feelings with Cameron and Renald and told them she was thinking about writing a letter to the star. When she got home, rather than a letter that would probably get lost in the fan mail, Selina started a poem about how it must be for the famous superstar...

Fear Of Falling Stars

I'M SITTING HERE WONDERING WHY
WHY SHE'S BUILT ME UP SO HIGH
WILL SHE EVER TEAR ME DOWN?
WILL SHE ALWAYS BE AROUND?
WILL I ONE DAY BE BELOW
EXTREME GREETINGS TO JUST "HELLO"?
I LOVE HER SO
BUT I'M AFRAID OF WHY
WHY SHE'S BUILT ME UP SO HIGH
MY EYES ARE COVERED SO SHE DOESN'T SEE
I'M LOOKING AT HER AS SHE'S STARING AT ME
I WATCH HER WITH A MORBID FEAR
OF REALLY LETTING HER GET NEAR
KNOWING SHE LOVES ANOTHER
SAYING SHE LOVES NO OTHER
I'M OVERWHELMED BY HER EMOTION
SKEPTICAL OF HER DEVOTION
MY BODY SHAKES AS SHE APPROACHES ME
I SING TO HER SO SHE CAN'T SEE
SHE WHISPERS THEN SHE STOPS AND STARES
SUDDENLY AS THOUGH WITHOUT A CARE
SHE SCREAMS AND SHOUTS AND PULLS HER HAIR
I DON'T UNDERSTAND HER REACTION
IS IT FROM PHYSICAL ATTRACTION?
EVEN THOUGH I CAN'T COMPREHEND
I PRAY IT'S JUST A PASSING TREND
SHE FILLS ME WITH A LITTLE PRIDE
HOW CAN I ESCAPE HER LOVE SO WIDE
BUT THROUGH MY PRIVATE LIFE INSIDE
IT'S THE ONLY PLACE I HAVE TO HIDE

(Continued)

HOW WILL I FARE WHEN SHE'S NOT AROUND?
WHO WILL PICK MY FALLEN STAR FROM THE GROUND?
MY ONLY WISH IS FOR ME
TO LIVE RELAXED AND COMFORTABLY
DOES SHE REALIZE, CAN SHE SEE?
I TOO AM HUMAN NOT A DEITY

100
$10,000
$10,000
$10,000
100

An Uncertain Rumor

"Aleatrice is pregnant," is what you've just heard from Jennifer. The talk becomes intense and before you realize it, you have unintentionally added a bit of unfounded information to the rumor. Aleatrice is your best friend and you don't really believe there is any truth to this accusation; nevertheless, if there is truth to it, this would certainly raise doubt and mistrust in your friendship because Aleatrice has not even told you that she and DeMario were having a sexual relationship.

You don't know how to approach the situation or even if you should mention it at all. You conclude that if Aleatrice is truly your friend, she'll soon confirm or deny the accusation.

DeMario and Shane came to pick you and Aleatrice up to go to the game. While you are waiting for Aleatrice to get back from the ladies' room, Jennifer comes up to you and blurts out, "Well, is she pregnant? Did you find out?" DeMario and Shane look at you in total disgust as if you were the hypocrite that you were just made to look like. In your attempt to explain to them that things weren't the way they seemed, Aleatrice rejoins the group. Very angered by what he just witnessed, DeMario says, "Sharron is there something you want to ask Aleatrice?"

What do you do? How do you respond? Here's what you're confronted with...

EXIT

Gossip

A FAMILIAR NAME CALLED
I DID NOT RESIST
I NOW KNOW I OUGHT NOT
HAVE LISTENED TO THIS
NOW FILLED ARE MY EARS
WITH MANY AN EMPTY WORD
OF A CLOSE COMPANION
BAD NEWS I INTENTIONALLY HEARD
NOW I HAVE HOLDING
WHAT I CANNOT BEAR
SHOULD I TELL ANOTHER
OR JUST BEWARE
DETAILS NO DOUBT OF THIS
WERE MUCH EXAGGERATED
FEARFUL AM I STILL
TO UNDERESTIMATE IT
CONFIDENCES WE MAY
NEVER AGAIN SHARE
TO PASS IT WILL I HURT
OR SOMEHOW SHOW I CARE
IF SOMEONE SUSPECTS
A FRIEND MAY FALL
TO SAY NOT A WORD
IS HE A FRIEND AT ALL?

A Sad Comedy

The night was young. Previous plans of going to see a movie were being elaborated on by the group of friends that usually hung together on Friday nights. The group always tried to take into consideration the different age groups and by doing so allowed everyone to voice his suggestion. After everyone had his input, a comedy was chosen that was suitable for everyone to see.

The cars trailed each other to the nearest theater only to find that the movie they had selected was not playing there. Again they had a brief discussion and all agreed to go to the mall which offered a variety of movies to see. Rachel and Rodney were the youngest in the circle of friends and also the most inquisitive. They noticed a more popular movie being played and the comedy then became less appealing. Arthalia was the oldest in the group so she made an attempt to keep the group together but by this time everyone had decided to go see what he or she wanted to see.

The next day Arthalia received an unpleasant phone call from Brenda, the mother of Rachel and Rodney, requesting that she no longer associate with her children. Arthalia was confused and asked Brenda why she was making such a request. Brenda's reply led Arthalia to believe that Rachel and Rodney had either falsely accused her of participating in something that she had not or that they had told their parent only half the truth to protect themselves from punishment.

In either case, Arthalia was deeply hurt and wrote down what she hoped to be only first reactions...

First Reactions

OVER SOMETHING I AM SADDENED
FOR MY HEART IS FILLED WITH VEX
BUT ALL THINGS HAVE A REASON
EITHER SIMPLE OR COMPLEX

OVER WHAT I WORRY MOST
ARE THE WORDS I WANT TO SAY
I AM DISPLEASED WITH MYSELF
FOR BEING LED TO FEEL THIS WAY

IT HAPPENED ON A FRIDAY NIGHT
WHILE DECIDING WHERE TO GO
A MOVIE WAS SELECTED
WE ALL AGREED ON ONE SHOW

BEING SHOVED FROM SIDE TO SIDE
WE WERE TAKEN BY SURPRISE
STANDING IN THE CROWD FOR SOME
A DIFFERENT MOVIE CAUGHT THEIR EYES

ALL OF US BEING OF AGE
FOR THE MOVIE WE WOULD SEE
TO STAY WAS OUR CHOICE
FOR THAT'S WHERE WE WISHED TO BE

OVER ACTIONS, THOUGHTS AND DEEDS
YOU YOURSELF SHOULD HAVE CONTROL
NOT ALWAYS PASSING THE BUCK
"I DID THIS WAY FOR I WAS TOLD"

WE WERE ALL OLD ENOUGH
EVEN TO KNOW WRONG FROM RIGHT
AN OBSERVATION OF THIS YOU MADE
WELL BEFORE YOU GOT HOME THAT NIGHT
"TAKE THE BLAME OFF OF ME.
WHERE YOU PUT IT I DON'T CARE!"
FIRST REACTIONS I UNDERSTAND
BUT DO YOU PLAN TO LEAVE IT THERE?

Chasing Dreams

Keith was the most popular guy in his neighborhood. All the girls were drawn to him because of his charm and good looks. The ladies were attracted to the deep respect he had for women. He was a gentleman, a trait that was very rare for a guy his age. The men liked him for his ability to 'get the job done.' He always spoke what was on his mind yet never seemed to be uncouth.

Leon was the smartest guy in his class. Because he was so smart, his classmates often mocked him as a method of intimidation. Leon wanted badly to be accepted by his classmates so as to make himself fit in with the crowd; Leon often found himself in trouble with the teacher for being the class clown. To Leon this was the only way he knew to get the pressure of being labeled a 'suck up' off of him.

Hector enjoyed solitude. For the most part, he was quiet and reserved. He found contentment in drawing nature scenes and listening to jazz. Understandably, the teachers loved him as a student and he had no problems being harried by the other classmates for this as did Leon. Despite Hector's shy nature, girls and guys both favored his company.

Keith, Leon and Hector, all possessing very diverse personalities causing them to be either liked or disliked by their neighbors, instructors or fellow classmates, were three very best friends. Their friendship had managed to survive several attacks from different peer groups. No one could quite put his finger on the thread that held these three together but their secret was simple. They had long ago made a resolve to accept themselves as who and what they were and this enabled them to accept each other the same way. They had made a pact that, rather than chase false dreams, they would enhance the assets they each exhibited. Their motto was: "I am a firm believer in what I believe."

Listen to their resolution...

False Happiness

I ONCE PONDERED OVER THIS
THOUGHT ABOUT IT NIGHT AND DAY
YES I WONDERED TO MYSELF
WHY DOES IT ALWAYS SEEM THIS WAY...
FALSE HAPPINESS FULL OF STRIFE—
IS NOT THIS THE CASE WITH LIFE
TO HAVE WHAT WE DO NOT WANT
AND TO LOVE WHAT WE DO NOT HAVE
THEN I MADE A RESOLUTION
AS FOR ME HERE'S WHAT I SAY
THINK ABOUT YOUR LIFE AHEAD
LEARN FROM THINGS OF YESTERDAY

PRE-JUDGING

In high school there were various groups called 'cliques.' It was very important to some people to belong to one of these groups. If one group turned you away, you just continued until you were accepted by another.

There were the brainiacs, the brawns, the preppies, the jocks; then there were the headbangers, the skaters, the poindexters, the nerds; finally there were the geeks and the buttheads. I guess it wasn't that bad. If you weren't smart, didn't dress well, weren't born with good looks, weren't athletic, then you could join the skaters or the headbangers. On the other hand, if you couldn't skate or get into the headbangers' music without getting a headache, you could always group with the buttheads and talk down the rest of them.

Personally, Dawn never wanted to be associated with any group. She appreciated her individuality and liked being known for herself as opposed to whom she hung with. She took a special interest in ones who had been rejected by certain groupies. Since Dawn bore characteristics that would qualify her for any of the popular groups, she had very high self- esteem. She used her abilities to help other people. She helped them with their schoolwork, coached them in dress and personal care, took them under her wing and helped build their self-confidence.

The problem was that after Dawn had done what she considered a good deed, one of the cliques would come and snatch her protege away because that person had become cool enough to be in their group. Time after time Dawn would watch a person she had considered a friend turn into a sour, heartless, self-centered groupie.

Immediately following every episode, Dawn would make a promise to her mother, who was unhappy with her actions, that she would stop catering to this type person. However, no sooner than the words would leave her mouth, another would come to her and Dawn just could not let the person feel unwanted or dejected.

When Dawn thought of the audacity that people had in putting themselves in a position to judge others, it made her very angry. She held the belief that intelligence was wasted on ignorance, and for this reason she refused to voice her opinion of such ones.

One day when Dawn was again feeling that her efforts were useless, Elise, one of the girls Dawn had lost to a clique, came back to visit her. Elise was ashamed of how she had treated Dawn and wanted to reconcile their friendship. Elise had discovered that having a genuine friend and confidante was more important than being popular. She told Dawn that she had the greatest admiration for her because of her strength to be her own person and not to conform under pressure.

Dawn accepted Elise's apology and together they analyzed the months of agony that they had experienced. Here's what they learned...

FRIENDSHIP PRIZE

WHEN I FAIL TO REALIZE
TRUE FRIENDS ARE HARD TO FIND
THE TREASURED MEMORY COMES TO ME
OF THE TIME I NEAR LOST MINE

WHEN FIRST THIS GIRL I MET I THOUGHT
SHE COULD NEVER BE MY FRIEND
OUR MINDS WERE QUITE IN CONTRAST
MINE ON PLEASURE HERS ON MEN

WHEN NEXT OUR TIPS DID TOUCH
GUESS GRADUAL CHANGE HAD SEEN IT'S END
OUR LIFE'S CONCEPTS LEANED FORWARD
I TOO HAD A MAN AS FRIEND

WHEN FEAR HAD BEEN REMOVED FROM US
AND TRUST COULD BE REVEALED
WE RELEASED OUR FEELINGS FROM THEIR CELLS
AND LABELED FRIENDSHIP SEALED

NOW GOOD OLD TIMES HAD BEEN DISPLAYED
AND HARDSHIPS OVERTHROWN
A PART CAME RIGHT INTO THE SCENE
THE PART I'D NEVER KNOWN

SO DISAPPOINTMENT PLAYED ITS ROLE
BUT UNDERSTANDING CAME ON STAGE
IT STIRRED IN FREEDOM, TRUST AND FEAR
AND SLOWLY BAKED IT INTO AGE

AND NOW WHEN GROWING CHANGE IS MADE
MY FRIEND AND I REALIZE
WE TOO MUST MAKE A CERTAIN CHANGE
TO WIN THE FRIENDSHIP PRIZE

Death Do Us Part

"No one will ever hurt me again!" is the cry for help that Latina shouted after her last broken relationship. She was determined that the next man in her life would commit to her and marry her. She had often listened to her father accuse her mother of 'trapping' him into marrying her by getting pregnant ; however, she knew that in her generation this wouldn't work because she had many friends with babies and no husbands.

In her desperation, Latina resorted to attempted suicide as a measure to create guilt on the part of Justin who had recently dumped her. Her ploy seemed effective because as soon as the word got out that "Latina tried to kill herself," Justin came back to her.

Latina was so happy! However, in her determination to achieve what she thought would bring her true satisfaction in life, she had risked everything that kept her together as a person. The grief she caused both family and friends was too overwhelming for her to deal with; therefore, she barricaded these feelings outside her heart so that they did not affect her at all.

Justin wore the face of a prisoner while Latina wore a smile that brought sadness to all who had loved and cared for her. They watched her day by day turn into an uncaring, man-hungry animal.

Had Latina found a happy, satisfying relationship with Justin? Did it matter that Justin was only glued to her by guilt? At last the monster that had captured her mind was revealed.

SELFISHNESS

OLDER WE HAVE GROWN
OUR URGE TO ACQUIRE
HAS OVERPOWERED REASON
HAS STRENGTHENED OUR DESIRE

THOUGH NATURAL DESIRING
THAT WHICH NOT POSSESSED
BY GAINING IS THERE JUSTICE
WHEN OTHERS ARE ABASHED?

TRY WE SHOULD RECALL
WHEN WE WERE BUT A LAD
WE SEEMED TO DO WITHOUT
THE THINGS WE NEVER HAD

GO BENEATH THE SURFACE
ALLOW YOUR HEART CONFESS
THAT WHICH IS NOW UNCOVERED
IS BITTER SELFISHNESS

Casanova Graduate

Fernell's body was well developed for her age. She had been dating Bobby, a suave senior, and the desire to please him was placed before anything else in her life. On occasion, several of Fernell's friends would tell her that Bob was playing her and advise her to ask him about it; however, she ignored the advice plus got upset with her friends for saying these things about Bobby.

Soon Fernell felt the truth of what was being said. She felt that she was losing him. Too embarrassed to now lean on her friends for support, she tried to deal with the situation alone. Little did Fernell know to what extent she had lost Bob until she received a wedding invitation with a letter from him, apologizing to her. He kindly explained that he planned to join the Navy directly after graduation. He needed a wife and unfortunately she was too young to be married. The wedding was to take place a week before graduation and it would mean a lot to him if she attended.

As soon as Fernell's friends heard about this, they were by her side. Fernell carried on in her usual manner and everyone was commenting on how well she accepted this fact. "Don't waste time worrying about things you cannot change," is what Fernell's mom kept telling her; nevertheless, her mom was stupefied by her daughter's unusual calmness. She suggested that Fernell not go to the wedding, but Fernell kept telling her mom she had to be there.

The day of the wedding, Fernell waited inside the restroom until she could hear the music playing. She then swallowed the bottle of pills that had accompanied her to the wedding and went and joined her friends in the audience. Their smiles of encouragement quickly faded as she drifted off...

The rescue squad rushed in and struggled to revive her. The sound of the siren drowned out the vows being made. The flashing lights disrupted the audience, causing them to turn their attention to the scene in back of them.

George was among the friends who had come with Fernell. As he looked on, he wondered, " Did Fernell really want to die or just hurt the man she loved as much as he hurt her?" He made a promise to himself never to play with another person's emotions. He also reckoned that if ever he were in a similar situation, he would get more involved as far as comforting his friends was concerned.

Fernell was rushed to the hospital in time to save her life; however, the prolonged lack of oxygen caused severe brain damage. She would remain in a childlike state for the rest of her life.

At graduation, the senior class gave this gift to the Casanova graduate...

As Fern Grows

TWAS NOT TOO LONG AGO
A MESSAGE SHE RECEIVED
QUITE BRIEF ON THE TELEPHONE RECORDER

IT SAID THAT SHE SHOULD KNOW
FOR SHE HAD BEEN DECEIVED
HER LOVER WAS ENGAGED TO ANOTHER

SHE MUST HAVE BEEN PERPLEXED
AS SHE WAS STANDING THERE
CARRYING ALONE THE WEIGHT OF HER WORLD

IT WAS TOO MUCH FOR HER
IT LEFT HER IN DESPAIR
FOR SHE WAS JUST A TEENAGE GIRL

SHE WAS ONE OF MANY
WHO GAVE ALL SHE COULD GIVE
WHO LOVED ONLY ONE MAN WITH ALL HER HEART

WHEN HE CHOSE TO END IT
HER STRONG DESIRE TO LIVE
WAS SHATTERED AND HER WHOLE LIFE FELL APART

THIS WAS A FATAL BLOW
NOW ALL HOPE WAS FADED
OF HER EVER LEADING A NORMAL ROLE

SHE WOULD BE AS A CHILD
JUST AS SHE PORTRAYED IT
NEVER AGAIN WOULD HURT ENTER HER SOUL

(continued)

SO TO BE LOVED AND LOVE NOT
MAY NOT SEEM QUITE SO BAD
THAT IS IF YOU'RE ON THE RECEIVING END

BUT TO THE GIVER OF THIS LOVE
IT IS SILENT PAIN THAT'S SAD
AND LONGED TO BE SHARED WITH A FRIEND

HOW DO I KNOW?
QUITE SIMPLE YOU SEE
THE SHE IS NOT SHE BUT ME

Anyone having thoughts of suicide or knowing of someone who talks of suicide, should let someone know without delay. Contact the suicide hotline for more information on suicide prevention and possible verbal or silent signs to look for.

A Message From Kimberly

All the girls had a crush on him. He knew what to say to each one to make her heart throb. To him and his buddies , it was harmless fun . "Which one of the 'little girls' would actually believe his proposal of marriage?" At age thirteen, "Wait until you're older" may seem like a long way off, yet they are very soon sixteen and ready to cash in on those promises.

Now that Kim had matured, the pain of reality was staring her right in the eyes and she had to cope with the truth that Andy had never planned to marry her. It infuriated her to think of the many promises he had made to her which he never intended to keep.

In Andy's endeavor to appease Kimberly, he thoughtlessly again encouraged her to wait a couple more years; however, the one thing that Kim was thankful for was that her crush had not crushed her spirit. Here is how she responded to Andy...

The King

THINGS HAD BEEN JUST FINE
THEY USUALLY WERE
PLENTY OF PARTIES
WITH FRIENDS WHO WOULD CARE
DAY IN AND DAY OUT
JUST A HAPPY ROUTINE
EACH DAY BETTER THAN BEFORE
WHO KNEW CIRCUMSTANCES UNFORESEEN?

I GUESS CHANGES HAVE TO COME
THINGS CAN'T ALWAYS STAY THE SAME
MAYBE LIFE WAS TOO GOOD
FOR FOOLS LIKE ME
IT WAS JUST A GAME

ALL MY DREAMS WERE COMING TRUE
UNFOLDING RIGHT BEFORE MY EYES
WHO WOULD KNOW THAT VERY SOON
MY DREAMS WOULD BE EMBITTERED LIES

WHEN SOMETHING'S LOST CAN IT BE FOUND?
CAN IT COME BACK BETTER THAN BEFORE?
IF ONLY TIME CAN TELL
WILL A HIDDEN TREASURE WASH UP ON THE SHORE?

"GOOD COMES FROM BAD"
IS WHAT I HEAR YOU SAY
IF THAT IS REALLY SO
MY LIFE WILL BE HAPPY ONE DAY

(continued)

IT WAS ALL GOING SO WELL
TO WHAT THINGS COULD HAVE LED
NOW IT'S JUST SWEET MEMORIES
AS I REMINISCE ON MY BED
SO MANY THINGS LEFT TO SAY
FEELINGS HANGING ON A STRING
STILL HOPES CAN SOAR AND DROWN IN ONE DAY
FOR BREAKING HEARTS, I KNOW THE KING

SO WHAT'S ON THE SCENE?
IS THAT WHAT I'M TO DO?
JUST SIT AROUND AND HOPE AND DREAM
AND WAIT TO HEAR FROM YOU?

AT GRANDMA'S HOUSE

The apartment was small; nevertheless, there always seemed to be enough room for the ten children and twenty-two grandchildren to come home to visit. The small city of Sylacauga in Alabama seemed to light up when my family came home. My grandmother Elnora, Big Mama as we called her, also welcomed her friends and neighbors over. Traffic in and out the house was a normal scene at Big Mama's house.

This was no special afternoon. School had been dismissed and we were all gathered at Big Ma's house in front of the big floor model TV. My attention drifted away from the scene as I heard talk of the war. My uncles, Bill and David, had both joined the military. Bill had dedicated over ten years of his life to the Army and thereby had chosen to make a career of it. David had been honorably discharged due to a war injury.

The conversation intensified with discussions as to whether it was more advantageous for my youngest uncles, Johnny and Jay, to go to college or to the military. Their brothers had received their college degrees while in the Army and therefore encouraged them to do likewise; however, Johnny and Jay argued that things had changed a lot since they were in school and their goal was to play college football.

Their final decision was to first go to college

and maybe later go to the Army to receive any additional benefits. Their strong conviction was in support of breaking down the racial barrier that had so long restricted them from making their own choices. Would they attend one of the few colleges that had been selected for them or would they challenge society's norm and enroll in a different school altogether?" Why shouldn't they go to the school of their choice? Why were things so divided in the world? What could people do together to tear down these barriers?

After a moment, I ran up the thirteen familiar stairs and got a pencil and paper. Sitting on Big Mama's bed, I began to write the solution that I thought was so simple. I wrote...

FIRST LOVE

LOVE BETWEEN THE WHITE AND BLACK
IS ALL CLOSED UP IN THE TINIEST SACK

SOMEONE WILL HAVE TO TAKE IT OUT
IF THEY KNOW WHAT LOVE'S ABOUT

LOVE IS WHAT GOD GAVE TO ADAM AND EVE
IT'S WHAT HE WANTED US ALL TO RECEIVE

HE ASSURED US IF EVERYONE LIVED BY THIS RULE
WHETHER WE ARE AT HOME, AT CHURCH, OR AT SCHOOL
"DO UNTO OTHERS AS YOU'D HAVE THEM DO TO YOU"
EVERYONE WOULD LOVE EVERYONE AND THEY'D
LOVE YOU TOO

I HOPE YOU ARE SEEING WHAT I WISH YOU TO SEE
THAT GOD DIDN'T MEAN FOR LOVE TO BE
RACES THINKING THEY'RE BETTER THAN ONE ANOTHER
FIGHTING AND KILLING THEIR GOD-GIVEN BROTHER

SO LET LOVE BETWEEN THE BLACK AND WHITE
BE LOOSED AND NOT KEPT SO TIGHT

LET THE FIRST LOVE THAT GOD GAVE YOU, SAVE YOU

The Runaway

Nikki lived at home with her mother and younger brother and sister. Her mother worked the night shift at her regular job, but she also had to work a part-time job during the day to make ends meet. Nikki was "Miss Mom" most of the time because even when her mother was home, she had to sleep to get rested for her next job.

Nikki had been comfortable in this role for many years. It made her very close to Tiffany and Tarek, her sister and brother. When people saw Nikki, they saw the 'tag-alongs' right there with her. She took them to the school games on Friday night, to the movies on Saturday, and to church on Sunday. Even though Nikki was teased by her friends for having to take her 'babies' with her everywhere she went, she continued doing it without complaining.

Greg was Nikki's friend. Although Greg often went places with Nikki, Tiffy and Tarek, this year was different. Greg wanted to take Nikki out on a real date without her sister and brother. Nikki didn't see a problem with that so she talked to her mom about it.

To Nikki's disappointment, her mother said she didn't feel comfortable leaving the kids home alone. They were still too young. Nikki reminded her mom that she was staying home with them alone when she was their age. "What made me old enough to keep them but them not old enough to keep themselves?" Unable to budge her mother's decision, Nikki made up her mind that it was time for her to leave.

One week had passed and Lena, Nikki's mom, was worried sick. Nikki's absence made Lena realize the heavy responsibility that she had unintentionally put on her little girl. All Lena wanted was for Nikki to come home so that she could have another chance at being her mother.

Another week passed with no word from Nikki. Lena tried to function as if everything was normal. She received a phone call from Terrence, her brother, discussing plans for the upcoming family reunion. "Ask Nikki if we can count on her to sing this year," were the words that caused Lena to break into tears.

No stone was left unturned in the intensified search for Nikki. Lena had a strong sense of security seeing her entire family join in the search for her daughter. Lena was a loner and had always tried to correct her problems without outside help but she realized that sometimes help from friends and family is a must.

Three days after the family had joined in the search for Nikki, she was found. She had ended up at her father's house in New York. Her father phoned Lena as soon as she got there to let her know she was safe; however, they agreed to let her stay there until she felt like she was ready to return home.

Sitting in the midst of the family reunion with Tiffany and Tarek on either side of her, Lena was again saddened by the empty seat reserved for Nikki. Terrence acted as master of ceremonies over the more than one hundred and fifty relatives who had shown up at the reunion.

Terrence made the announcement that the time had come for special recognition and each family member proudly announced new births, graduations, anniversaries, promotions, special awards and weddings. Now it was time for the grand finale—a song written by one of the children. Chills ran down Lena's spine as she tried not to think about her little girl who would have been singing this song.

The audience waited with keen anticipation to see who would sing the song. They were thrown off when all the nieces and nephews went up on the stage to perform. Lena watched the performance with tears in her eyes. Very soon the entire audience joined her as they heard the strong, familiar voice of Nikki ring out from among her cousins. Lena's tears of sadness turned to tears of joy as she ran to embrace her daughter.

It was a family reunion to be remembered. It made everyone present realize that each member played an important role in making a family circle. With just one missing, the circle would be incomplete. Here are the words that reunited Nikki with Lena, Tiffany and Tarek...

FAMILY CIRCLE

A MOTHER LISTENS AND UNDERSTANDS
WHEN WE ARE IN DEEP DESPAIR
A FATHER HELPS TO LIFT THE PAIN
WHEN THE HURT SEEMS TOO HARD TO BEAR
A SISTER'S SMILE CAN MAKE THINGS RIGHT
SO WE KNOW THERE'S A BRIGHT TOMORROW
A BROTHER MAKES OUR HEART FEEL LIGHT
BY SHARING OUR BURDEN OF SORROW
AUNTS AND UNCLES WILL HEAR US SPEAK
WHEN WE FEEL NO ONE ELSE WILL LISTEN
GRANDPARENTS WILL CERTAINLY KEY US IN
ON "THE GOOD OLE TIMES" WE'VE BEEN MISSING
NIECES AND NEPHEWS AND COUSINS AND SUCH
WILL ALWAYS RESPECT US AND LOVE US SO MUCH
SO WHENEVER IN LIFE WE MAY GO WRONG
OUR FAMILY's SUPPORT WILL KEEP US STRONG

To Will With Love

Cecie and Will had the kind of friendship that many people only fantasize about. They valued their companionship so much that despite romantic feelings for each other they would not allow themselves to become intimate for fear this would complicate things. The underlying beauty of their relationship was that when you saw them together their affection was so apparent that people assumed "for anyone to be that happy they had to be romantically involved."

The secret to their successful friendship was simple: each one accepted the other as he or she was and they showed this by constantly trying to make the other one comfortable. Sometimes they would get irritated with each other but it was usually due to indecisiveness such as: "Where do you want to go?" "Oh, wherever you like is fine with me." "Well, I want to go where you want to go." "I'll go wherever you chose." They usually resorted to a third party making the decision.

After graduation, Will proposed to Cecie. They were both going to go to college and Cecie had heard many stories of women never finishing college because of getting married, then pregnant. She didn't want this to happen to her; therefore she refused.

After a couple of years, Will again proposed to

Cecie. This time he also told her that he was going to join the military. Again Cecie thought it best to wait. Even though they both relocated to different states, they maintained their friendship over the phone.

Another five years passed and Will once again asked Cecie to marry him, to be the mother of his kids. After this refusal, Will let Cecie know that this would be the last time he would propose to her. Cecie thought long and hard about life without her confidant. There was no doubt in her mind that he loved her and she loved him as well; however, her reasons for not wanting to be married were deeper than she could even share with him.

Cecie allowed another year to pass without giving Will any indication as to whether or not she planned to spend her future with him. Finally, she got worried that she had not heard from him. She had no way of getting in touch with him due to his traveling, so she just had to wait and pray that he would soon write or call her.

The phone call soon came, but not from Will, rather from Cecie's mother. "Will's getting married," her mother happily told her. "I always liked Will. I sort of wished you had married him." Cecie's mother continued talking, not knowing she was stabbing her daughter with each word she was saying.

That night Cecie unsealed the letter she had written to Will a year ago. The happiness she was looking for in a mate is well described in the private wedding vows that she wrote but never mailed to Will with love...

My Wedding Promise

MY LOVE FOR YOU I HAVE EXPRESSED
AND YOU YOUR LOVE FOR ME
WE CHERISHED EACH OTHER
PASSED THE TEST
AND NOW WE BOTH AGREE
THAT TIME HAS COME
TO DO THE THINGS
FOR WHICH WE HAVE A FONDNESS
OUR SORROW, LAUGHTER, JOY AND PAIN
COMBINED INTO OUR ONENESS
IN LIFE NOW I DO ALL THINGS
TO PLEASE AND SATISFY YOU
RAIN OR STORM
MY PROMISE REMAINS
ALWAYS TO STAND BY YOU
TOGETHER WE CAN WEATHER
ANYTHING THAT COMES OUR WAY
TOGETHER WE CAN MAKE IT HAPPEN
EACH AND EVERY DAY
AS WE BECOME TO EACH OTHER
A HUSBAND AND A WIFE
MAY OUR HEARTS BE UNITED
AS WE ENTER OUR NEW LIFE

ABOUT THE AUTHOR

It is not the intention of the author to offer as valid therapeutic solutions any suggestions made in this book. The author has chosen to create realistic scenarios only to convey the message to the reader that someone, somewhere has experienced the emotions that you may be feeling at the present time; heretofore, if you have felt that there is no one you can talk to about your feelings, by reading some of the life experiences of others you may still bear the comfort "YOU ARE NOT ALONE."

There are hotline numbers easily accessible in your local areas for persons needing to talk to someone in the unfortunate event of severe depression due to loneliness, rejection, injustice, fear or anxiety which may be contributing to thoughts of running away, criminal acts of violence and more seriously, suicide. Reach out for help.